THE WORLD'S SMARTEST ANIMALS

HORSES

by Ruth Owen

WINDMILL BOOKS

New York

Published in 2012 by Windmill Books, An Imprint of Rosen Publishing
29 East 21st Street, New York, NY 10010

Editor for Ruby Tuesday Books Ltd: Mark J. Sachner
U.S. Editor: Sara Antill
Designer: Emma Randall
Consultant: Kelly Taylor BSc(hons) BCaBA EBQ, www.equinebehaviourconsultant.co.uk

Cover, 1, 5, 9, 10–11 (main), 13, 19, 20–21, 22–23, 25, 28–29, 30 © Shutterstock; 6–7, 8, 17 © Wikipedia Creative Commons (public domain); 11 (top) © Kelly Taylor; 14–15 © Alamy; 25 (top) © Todd Sumlin; 27 © Erik S. Lesser.

Library of Congress Cataloging-in-Publication Data

Owen, Ruth, 1967–
 Horses / by Ruth Owen.
    p. cm. — (The world's smartest animals)
 Includes index.
 ISBN 978-1-61533-378-3 (library binding) — ISBN 978-1-61533-418-6 (pbk.) —
ISBN 978-1-61533-475-9 (6-pack)
 1. Horses—Juvenile literature. I. Title.
 SF302.O94 2012
 636.1—dc22

                                    2011013827

Manufactured in the United States of America

CPSIA Compliance Information: Batch #RTS1102WM: For Further Information contact Windmill Books, New York, New York at 1-866-478-0556

CONTENTS

OUR FRIEND THE HORSE

A man is in trouble in the ocean.
He is drowning!
Two members of the police force are on the shore.
They jump into the water and swim to the drowning man.
The brave police save the man's life!

You might think these members of the police force were two brave human officers. One of the rescuers, however, was a horse named Bertie! When the police horse's rider asked him to swim out to the drowning man, brave Bertie didn't hesitate.

Around the world, thousands of horses work as police horses. These smart animals also work on farms, take part in sports, and give their human owners hours of fun and friendship. Some horses are even trained to be support animals for people with disabilities!

Horses have very good memories. They will often remember how to do a task that they were taught to do many years before. They will also remember people who frightened or mistreated them, as well as the people who showed them love and respect.

HORSE SKILLS

A young foal shows off the speed that one day could make it a champion racehorse!

Show jumping is a popular sport.

ALL ABOUT HORSES

Horses are mammals that eat grass and other plants. They are part of an animal family that includes donkeys and zebras.

Most of the 60 million horses in the world are **domesticated**. This means they live alongside people as pets or working animals.

The only truly wild horses alive today are Przewalski's horses. These horses live wild in Mongolia, in Asia. In 1945, Przewalski's horses were

extinct in the wild. There were just 31 living in zoos. The zoos bred the horses, and by the early 1990s, their numbers had risen to around 1,500. **Conservation groups** took some of the horses to live wild in Mongolia. No one knew if the zoo horses would survive as wild animals. The plan worked, however, and now there are around 400 Przewalski's horses living wild.

Around the world, many different types of horses, such as mustangs in the United States, live wild. These horses are not truly wild, however. They are feral. This means they were once domesticated. These horses escaped from their owners, or were let go, and now live a wild life.

HORSE SKILLS

Przewalski's horses have never been domesticated by people.

THE HORSE AS A PREY ANIMAL

Horses are naturally **prey** animals. The ancestors of today's pet horses had to avoid meat-eating **predators**, such as bears, mountain lions, and humans.

Horses have very large eyes that allow them to keep watch for danger in almost every direction without moving their heads. Horses can run fast to escape from danger. They can also rear up away from a threat.

When a person first puts a saddle on a young horse, it might buck. This is a smart reaction for a prey animal. The horse's ancestors had to be ready to buck off an attacking mountain lion. Rearing up at a fluttering plastic bag in a hedge can be frightening to a horse's human rider. The horse is just protecting itself and its human friend from a sudden unknown danger, though.

A horse will sleep facing a getaway route!

Horses can get some of the sleep they need while standing up. This means they are ready to run if a predator approaches. Horses have **ligaments** and **tendons** that allow them to lock their legs in place. They can then relax their muscles without falling over!

HORSE SKILLS

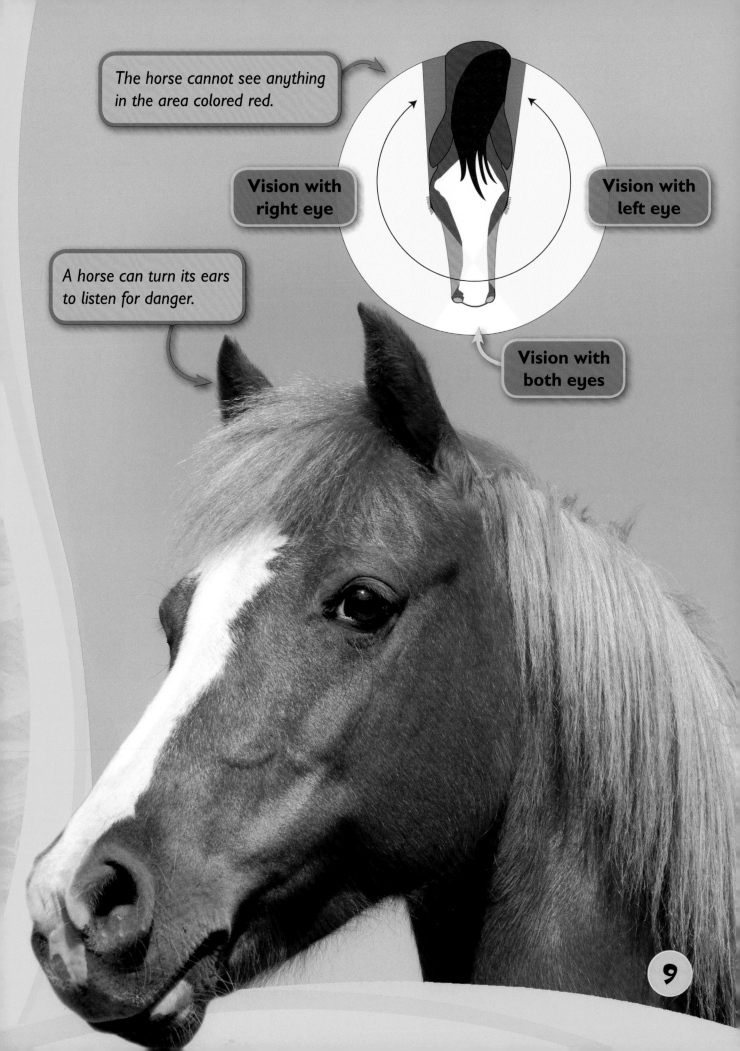

The horse cannot see anything in the area colored red.

Vision with right eye

Vision with left eye

A horse can turn its ears to listen for danger.

Vision with both eyes

9

LiFE iN A HERD

A horse may live in a stable and have human friends, but deep inside it wants to live with other horses and be part of a herd.

In the wild, a herd of horses will include adult females, called mares, their foals, and young males and females. The leader of the herd is an old, **experienced** mare. The lead mare's job is to find food and water for the group. She will also show the herd which way to run if they are in danger. The herd follows its leader because they trust and respect her. This is because she has shown them over time that she makes good decisions.

Each herd also has an adult male called a stallion. He spends time within the herd and on the edge of the group, ready to fight off predators.

A herd of horses

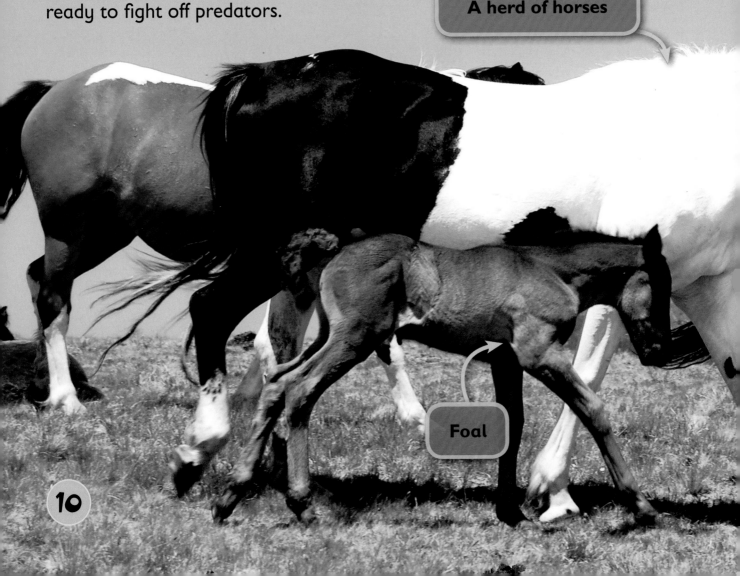

Foal

A horse sleeps while another herd member keeps watch.

Horses need to have some deep sleep. To get deep sleep, a horse must lie flat on the ground. Living in a herd allows horses to lie down and relax. While some herd members sleep, one of the adult horses will stand guard and watch for predators.

HORSE SKILLS

PLAYMATES AND WORKMATES

Horses have been domesticated for around 6,000 years.

Horses are smart, so they can be trained to do things. They want to be part of a herd, but they can build strong friendships with people. When a person gives protection, kindness, and respect to a horse, the horse can learn to trust that person. It will feel safe enough to do what the person asks of it.

Before people had gas-powered vehicles, horses pulled carts, buses, and farm machines. Horses also pulled fire engines. Experienced fire horses knew that when they heard the fire bells ring, they should go to the fire engine and wait to be harnessed up!

Horse racing is a popular sport. Racehorses are **thoroughbred** horses. They can run faster than 50 miles per hour (80 km/h)!

In **medieval** times, fighting men called knights fought for kings and lords in wars. Knights fought on fierce, brave horses called destriers. The horses were trained to bite and kick enemies during battles.

HORSE SKILLS

WAR HORSES

Millions of soldiers fought and died in World War I. Millions of horses went to war, too.

Horses were used to pull heavy guns, transport weapons and food, and carry away wounded and dying soldiers. Horses were also ridden into battle as **cavalry** horses.

The British Army did not have enough horses, so British families had to send their pet and working horses to war! Between 1914 and 1917, the United States also sent 1,000 horses each day to the British Army in Europe.

Over eight million horses died in World War I. Even though they were hungry and scared, the horses worked hard. They charged into battle surrounded by gunfire. After the war, many soldiers talked about the horses' bravery.

Many WWI soldiers were just teenagers, not experienced soldiers. The young men did not want to show the other soldiers they were homesick and afraid of dying. They would often tell their troubles to their trusted horse friends. The horses were a great comfort to the soldiers.

HORSE SKILLS

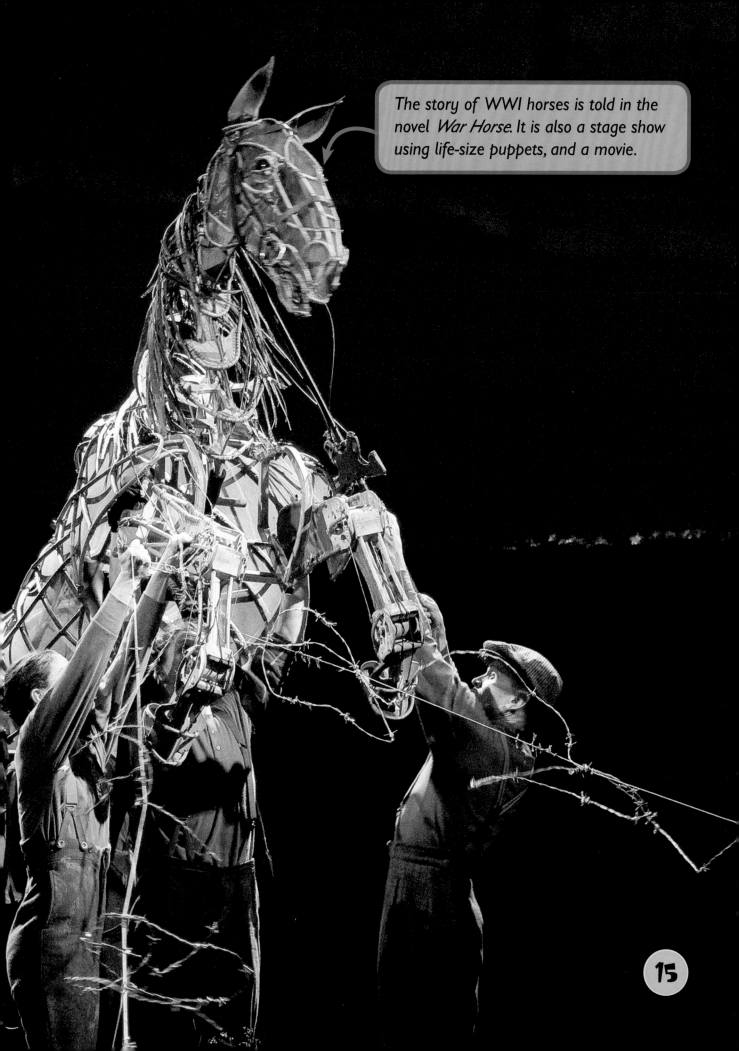

The story of WWI horses is told in the novel *War Horse*. It is also a stage show using life-size puppets, and a movie.

A DAY iN THE LiFE OF A POLiCE HORSE

Police horses are trained to be calm and confident when surrounded by noisy vehicles, shouting crowds, and even explosions!

An average day for a police horse starts with a breakfast of horse feed, hay, and vegetables. The horse's rider or a stable worker will wash its mane and tail, groom its coat, and put on its saddle and other riding equipment. The horse then rides in a trailer to where it will be working that day.

A police horse's day might include controlling city traffic. The horse might also help keep crowds under control during a parade or sporting event. Police horses can also chase criminals in places where police cars cannot go, such as in traffic jams and down alleys!

Young police horses go on patrol with an older, experienced horse. The older horse will show the youngster how to behave and give it confidence.

Police horses are trained to use their bodies to gently move people in large crowds. They are also trained not to step on people's feet! The police say that one police horse is more effective at crowd control than 10 officers on foot.

HORSE SKiLLS

A police horse and rider in London

PADDY, THE HORSE HERO

Paddy the Clydesdale horse lived with his owner, Mike Salmon, in Victoria, Australia. Paddy had been a police horse, and Mike had been his police officer rider.

In 2009, Victoria suffered terrible bush fires. One night, Mike saw fires coming toward his house. He decided to let his sheep and goats and Paddy out of their pens so they would not be trapped. Mike was hosing down his house and checking for embers, which are small burning pieces that could start a new fire. Then, he saw something amazing!

Paddy had rounded up the other animals, and they were taking cover under his huge body. Burning embers were falling all around, but Paddy didn't stop protecting the sheep and goats. Brave Paddy, Mike, and the other animals all survived the fire!

Clydesdales are a breed of very large, strong horses. They were bred for pulling farm equipment, such as plows. Clydesdales are used by the British Army in parades and ceremonies. These horses carry a rider and two silver drums. Each drum weighs 68 pounds (31 kg).

HORSE SKILLS

A team of Clydesdales in a parade

SO HOW SMART ARE HORSES?

Millions of horse owners can tell stories that show how smart their horse friends are!

Spending time in a stable is not natural for a horse. It can also be boring. Some horses learn how to undo the bolts and latches on their stable doors. Then they can escape to eat grass or see their horse friends!

One owner tells of a horse whose leg became trapped in a wire fence. If the horse had struggled and pulled, it would have seriously damaged its leg. The horse did the smart thing. It waited patiently on three legs until human help arrived.

Some horses even seem to know what time of day it is, and when their owner will arrive to see them. They might know this by looking at the position of the Sun in the sky.

Horses use their mouths and noses to open bolts on their stables.

HORSE SKILLS

A horse is unable to see a fence or a jump when it gets really close to it. Horses have to remember how high and wide obstacles are, and jump over them from memory!

BEAUTIFUL JIM KEY

Beautiful Jim Key was a horse people said could spell!

Jim's owner, Bill Key, had been a slave. Throughout his life, Bill had learned to work with animals. As a free man, he traveled the country with Jim. Bill used kindness and patience to train Jim. He taught Jim to perform stunts that involved spelling, math, telling time, and even using a cash register.

Jim's skills soon became a big attraction! Around 10 million Americans saw Jim perform in theaters and at fairs. Two million children signed Jim's pledge to be kind to animals.

Could Jim really spell and do math? No one knows for sure. One thing is certain, though. Whether Jim could do these things or was performing as part of a clever trick, he had to be one very, very smart horse!

HORSE SKILLS

Bill Key and Jim spread the word that people should be kind to animals and to each other. They raised money for **animal welfare groups**. They also raised money to help educate African Americans and to help children who were disabled or living in poverty.

A B C

TiNY HORSE HELPERS

Over one million people in the United States are blind. Some of these people have a Seeing Eye dog. Now, some people are using a guide horse!

Miniature horses are being trained to guide blind people. Some blind people might choose a guide horse because they are riders and love horses! A person might also want a guide who will be a companion for over 30 years. Horses live for a lot longer than dogs.

Guide horses live in a stable with a small corral outside the owner's home. When a guide horse is working, it will lead its owner to the office, to shopping malls, and into restaurants.

Guide horses can be trained to get into taxis and onto subways and buses. They are even allowed to fly on airplanes!

HORSE SKILLS

Horses have hard hooves that can slide on slippery floors in stores and shopping malls. Guide horse owners can buy tiny sneakers for their horses to wear to stop them from slipping! Unlike metal horseshoes, these sneakers don't set off alarms in airports!

A guide horse takes a train ride with its owner.

The guide horse is wearing horse sneakers.

After work, it's time for some grass and fun in the corral!

GUiDE HORSE TRAiNiNG

Guide horse owners rely on their horses to keep them safe. Each guide horse receives up to one year of training.

Being a guide horse is not a natural way for a horse to live. A horse would not normally ride in taxis or go to places such as shopping malls. Not all miniature horses are able to do the job.

Like police horses, guide horses are trained to be unafraid around crowds, moving vehicles, and loud noises. Horses can make good guide animals because they are naturally on the lookout for danger. When in traffic, the horse's all-round vision helps it look out for moving cars.

The owner and horse will become close to each other, like a small herd. The horse will never wander away from its herd!

To work indoors, a guide horse must be housebroken. When it needs to go outside to go to the bathroom, it is trained to make soft, whinnying noises and paw at the door with its hoof!

HORSE SKILLS

This guide horse is traveling on an airplane!

HORSES NEED OUR HELP

For millions of people, horses are well-cared-for friends, family members, or workmates. Sadly, not all people are kind to horses.

Animal welfare groups investigate many reports of cruelty to horses. Sometimes they have to rescue large numbers of horses from just one farm. These horses might be hungry, hurt, or sick. How can you help?

Speak out! If you see a horse being treated badly, report it to an animal welfare group.

Help out! Donate some of your allowance to an organization that is helping horses. Ask a grown-up if you can visit a horse rescue center and ask what help they need.

HORSE SKILLS

Rescue organizations can give abused horses a new life. An ex-racehorse was found not being given enough food to eat. Another horse was abandoned by its owner and got stuck under a fence. Both horses were rescued and made a fresh start as police horses in the Los Angeles County Sheriff's Department!

GLOSSARY

animal welfare groups
(A-nuh-mul WEL-fer GROOPS)
Organizations that carry out work
to stop the mistreatment of animals.
They might work with farm animals,
pets, or animals in zoos to make sure
the animals are treated with respect
and have good living conditions.

cavalry (KAL-vuh-ree)
The units in an army that had soldiers
on horseback. Today, cavalry units use
vehicles such as tanks.

conservation group
(kon-sur-VAY-shun GROOP)
An organization that does work
to protect the natural world from
damage by humans. The group might
campaign to protect a habitat or
a type of wild animal.

domesticated
(duh-MES-tih-kayt-ed)
Raised to live with people.

experienced (ik-SPEER-ee-entst)
Wise, with knowledge of how to
do things that has been gathered
over a long period of time.

extinct (ik-STINGKT)
No longer existing.

ligament (LIH-guh-ment)
A tough band of tissue that connects
two or more bones together.

mammal (MA-mul)
A warm-blooded animal that has a
backbone and hair, breathes air, and
feeds milk to its young.

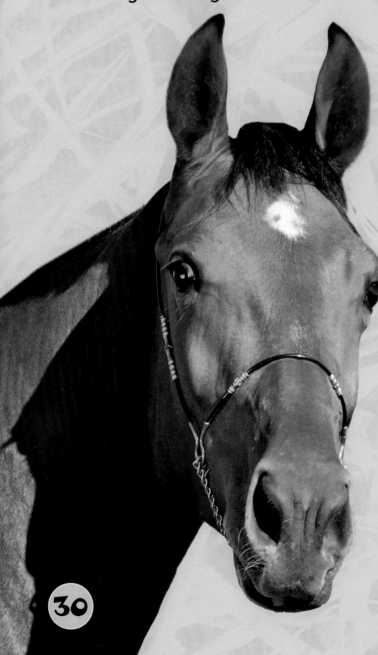

medieval (mee-DEE-vul)
Having to do with the Middle Ages, the years from A.D. 500 to A.D. 1450.

predator (PREH-duh-ter)
An animal that hunts and kills other animals for food.

prey (PRAY)
An animal that is hunted by another animal as food.

tendon (TEN-dihn)
A tough cord or band of tissue that connects a muscle to a bone.

thoroughbred (THER-oh-bred)
A breed of horse bred especially for racing. Thoroughbreds are fast and very lively.

World War I
(WURLD WOR WUN)
The war fought between the Allies and the Central powers from 1914 to 1918.

WEB SITES

For Web resources related to the subject of this book,
go to: www.windmillbooks.com/weblinks
and select this book's title.

READ MORE

Milbourne, Anna. *Horses and Ponies*. London: Usbourne, 2007.

Momatiuk, Yva and John Eastcott. *Face to Face with Wild Horses*. Des Moines, IA: National Geographic Children's Books, 2009.

Rockwood, Leigh. *Horses are Smart!*. Super Smart Animals. New York: PowerKids Press, 2010.

INDEX